TRAINS! HOW DO THEY WORK (ELECTRIC AND STEAM)?
Trains for Kids Edition

Children's Cars, Trains & Things That Go Books

All Rights reserved. No part of this book may be reproduced or used in any way or form or by any means whether electronic or mechanical, this means that you cannot record or photocopy any material ideas or tips that are provided in this book.

Copyright 2016

HAVE YOU BEEN ON A TRAIN JOURNEY?

In this book, you will get to know more about the wonderful machines that can take you from place to place.

Let's feed your natural curiosity about trains. How do they work?

WHAT MAKES THIS AMAZING TRANSPORTATION MOVE?

Trains were invented to transport passengers and goods along tracks. Trains come in different kinds for different purposes and environments.

Different energy sources are used to run and power trains. These energy sources are steam, diesel and electricity.

The first steam engine was built by Thomas Savery in 1698. It was improved in the mid-1800s by James Watt. People found it very useful.

Through the 19th century, steam locomotives were developed.

Steam-powered train engines were popular from the mid-1800s to the early 1900s.

In the 20th century, the use of diesel and electric locomotives were developed and replaced the steam locomotives.

In earlier times, before the advent of internal combustion engines, steam engines were used to move trains, boats and ships.

In a steam engine, energy from heat is transformed to mechanical energy. The steam enters a cylinder or a chamber in which a piston moves. Then, it pushes the piston back and forth.

The movement of the pistons gets passed to the rods, and from the rods to the wheels so they turn and the engine moves forward. A steam engine works like a bubbling teapot.

Coals or chunks of wood are loaded into the steam engine's fire box. The fire causes the water in the water tank to boil. In the boiling process, steam is produced.

The steam produces pressure which moves the pistons. When the piston moves, the rods and the wheels also move. By these, the train pushes forward.

Electric and diesel trains were developed from the 1940s to the 1960s. They replaced steam engines in different countries.

An electric locomotive is powered by electricity. Electric motors are used to drive the wheels.

The use of electricity to power trains lessens air pollution. They are known for more efficient performance.

Electric locomotives are more reliable than diesel or steam locomotives. People prefer them, for they are cleaner, quieter and faster.

High-speed trains are powered by electricity. The use of electric locomotives means no engine and exhaust noise.

Therefore, there is less mechanical noise. They are also easier on the tracks.

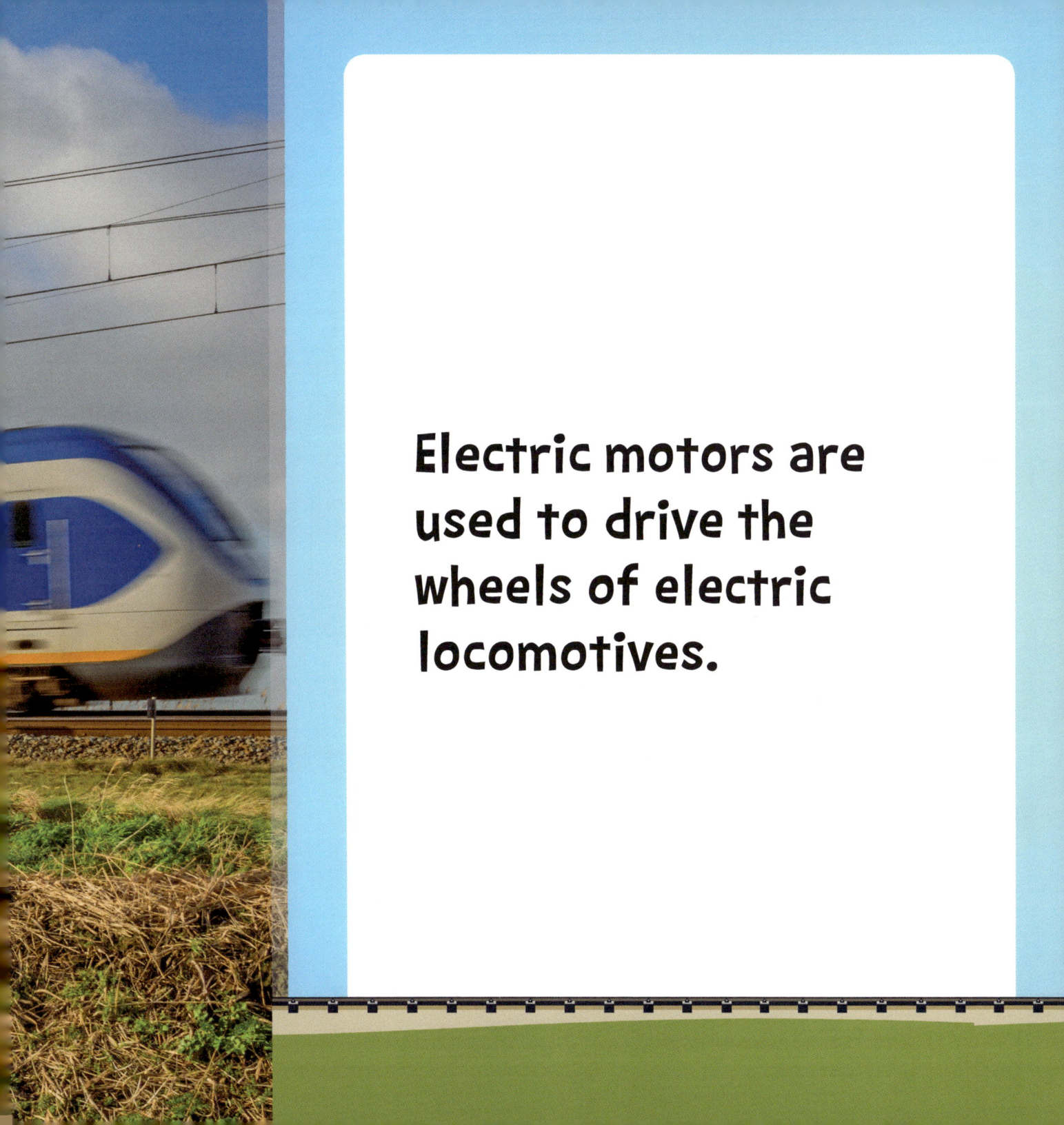

Electric motors are used to drive the wheels of electric locomotives.

Some electric trains get electricity from overhead cables. Some get power from third rails on the track.

Building the rails that carry electric current is very expensive.

Electric locomotives are advantageous for trains with frequent stops.

These are used in areas with advanced rail networks and on high-speed lines.

Overhead lines or third rails, control systems, and power substations are required for using electric locomotives.

Trains can take us many places. They are known to be one of the cheapest means of transportation.

Printed in Great Britain
by Amazon